A Gifted New Author

"Diane Haworth is a profoundly gifted new author. I cannot recommend this book highly enough. It is a true gem in its genre and a 'must read' for anyone who is seeking to better their lives."

- Dr. Todd Michael, Artist, Author of
The Evolution Angel and Physician (retired)

A Beacon of Hope

"Diane Haworth is an extraordinary human being. Her conscious commitment to deepen her loving expression in every aspect of her life is a beacon of hope for all who know her. If you read her book, you are sure to be blessed by her insights and guidance."

- Dianne Eppler Adams, Spiritual Mentor and Author of
Conscious Footsteps: Finding Spirit in Everyday Matters

Incredible Insight and Wisdom

"It is always a pleasure to see someone's destiny unfold. Diane brings her incredible insight and wisdom to life with her words and in the end, we are inspired by her."

-Alison Baughman, Numerologist, Visible by Numbers and Author of
Speaking to Your Soul: Through Numerology

Contagious and Inspirational

"Diane's energy is contagious and inspirational. She has a toolbox to fit the needs of everyone with whom she works. She is an expansive, creative, sensitive thinker that helps you get in touch with what is important on the inside, so that you can become all you are meant to be on the outside. She is all about infinite possibilities, a joy to be around."

-Donusia Lipinski, Immigration Lawyer,
Blue Ridge Immigration Law Center

Her Insights Are Amazing

"Working with Diane is an incredible experience. Her insights are amazing, but her real talent lies in her ability to energize and empower others. She is always able to show me exactly the right path to get me where I want to go."

-Harry J. Boyd, Security Consultant and Author

A Brilliant, Healing Presence

"Diane Haworth is a brilliant, healing presence and her work rocks!"

-Amber Valentyne, Entrepreneur

A Dose of JOY in My Life

"Diane is a wonderful coach, mentor and friend. She can pinpoint a problem that you never realized was the one thing holding you back and offer solutions. Seeing her monthly is getting a dose of JOY in my life. She has helped me tremendously."

- Caryn Moya Block, Amazon Bestselling
Paranormal Romance Author

A True Gift

"Making the decision to work with Diane has had an incredible impact on my life in the past year. Through her coaching and guidance, I was able to evaluate the current state of my life and strategically set goals to achieve the success and happiness I desired. With Diane's consulting, I have experienced abundance in ways that I could have never dreamed. She has a true gift and it's an honor to work with her."

-Allison B. Brincefield, Entrepreneur

See Love in Everything

"I was at a place in my life where I was either going to see Diane or I was going to get medication. I'm thankful I chose Diane. She taught me to see love in everything. That's a much better side effect."

-Nicolle Jones, Community Advocate

How to Choose Love When You Just Want to Slap Somebody

DIANE L HAWORTH

BALBOA.
PRESS

A DIVISION OF HAY HOUSE

Balboa Press books may be ordered through booksellers or by contacting:

Balboa Press
A Division of Hay House
1663 Liberty Drive
Bloomington, IN 47403
www.balboapress.com
1 (877) 407-4847

Printed in the United States of America.

ISBN: 978-1-4525-1493-2 (sc)
ISBN: 978-1-4525-1494-9 (e)

Library of Congress Control Number: 2014908817

Balboa Press rev. date: 8/4/2014

We are created in love, from love to live love.

Contents

Acknowledgements xi
Why I Wrote This Book xv
This Book is for You! xix

Chapter 1: Meditate! 1
Chapter 2: The Power of Gratitude 12
Chapter 3: You Are What You Think....................... 22
Chapter 4: What If Life is Working for You?............ 41
Chapter 5: What Does Love Look Like Here?
            How Does Love Move Me Forward? 48
Chapter 6: Living in the Now 54
Chapter 7: Release, Relax and Accept 61

Take Thoughtful Action: Choose to Live Love 77
About the Author 81

Acknowledgements

I FEEL SO many thank yous are appropriate for this book and I hope this listing reflects my gratitude for the support I've received. This represents only a few of the many important people and relationships that have helped me on my path. It's in no particular order. Whether they're listed here or not, I sincerely appreciate everyone who has touched my life.

Thank you to my darling husband Joe for his love, patience and support of me always (whether he understood what I was doing or not), to Mom and Dad for giving me my foundation, my brother Bill and sister-in-law Ann for being a constant grounding presence and always offering a respite at their loving home. Thank you to my sister Kathy for believing in me and coming with me on this spiritual journey as well as acting as a business and spiritual advisor. Thank you to my daughter Stephanie, her husband Evan and my son Kyle, who teach me daily about unconditional love. Thanks to Jason and Becky for being beautiful reflections of their father Joe and being part of my family. Many thanks go to my extended family that were supportive and encouraged me during the writing process. Thank you to my "adopted brother" Harry Boyd for his constant love and support of me and my family. My appreciation and love for friend Sharon Blum is beyond words...

thanks for teaching me about handling new love, marriage, kids and life!

I am grateful for the early teachings I received at my Presbyterian church in my small Virginia hometown. Although my understanding of the Divine has changed over the years, I'm thankful for my spiritual introduction to God's loving presence in my life and to the wonderful people I met there. Thank you to the church pastors for the spiritual lessons they taught me.

Thanks to kindred spirit Robin Knies, my friend who early on never questioned the unconventional topics and techniques I discussed with her and used her own curiosity to propel us both forward. I am grateful for friend Faye Richardson and her husband Bill, who supported my work and were always open to finding and sharing new ways to grow. Thank you to Nicolle Jones, Johnetta Pruitt, Triv Towery, Peter Fakoury, Donusia Lipinski, Anita Sutherland and the Sutherland family, Marianne Clyde and Alice Maher, who all embody love and inspire me with your actions. Thank you to Linda Lieving, who was my "rock" during a turbulent time in my life and gave me my first Louise Hay book, *You Can Heal Your Life*, for Christmas 1999.

Thank you to my author friends Shari Jaeger Goodwin, Caryn Moya Block and Dianne Eppler Adams for your love, support and encouragement.

Thank you to my coach and mentor Dr. Todd Michael, who helped bring this book to press and to my spiritual coach Rev. Joyce Liechenstein, Ph.D. for introducing us. Special thanks to my book coach Donna Kozik and editor Nancy Griffin-Bonnaire for keeping me on track.

Thanks also to business coach Ivy Stirling and to my previous coaches for your encouragement and support of this project. Thanks to Alice Maher, Sarah Steed, Ana Maria Siccardi and Petra Mercier for sharing your healing expertise as well. A very special thank you to Max Simon and Jeffrey Van Dyk who shifted my understanding of how I can best serve others through my business. Thank you for helping me create an exciting business that I love.

I'm grateful for all the authors I studied over the years. I especially appreciate the works of Louise Hay, Dr. Robert Holden, Gregg Braden, Eckhart Tolle, Dr. Deepak Chopra, Rhonda Byrne, Dr. Michael Bernard Beckwith, Anthony Robbins, Zig Ziglar, Dr. Jack Canfield, Dr. Wayne Dyer, Diana Cooper, Vianna Stibal, Marlo Morgan, Ted Andrews and Stuart Wilde.

Thanks to Rev. Beth Chadsey for teaching me Reiki and expanding my inner world. To the fabulous people who have been my teachers, mentors and friends: Janis Ericson, Melissa Feick, Catherine Rosek, John J. Oliver, Alison Baughman, Miranda Powell and my friends at the Aquarian Bookshop in Richmond, Virginia. Much love and gratitude goes to Amy Twiss and my Aussie buddy Susanne Marie for their steadfast support and for bringing me greater understanding of metaphysical and spiritual tools. To Theta founder Vianna Stibal and her husband Guy, I am eternally grateful for the dedication of you and your family to bring ThetaHealing® to the planet. Thank you!

Thank you to Sherri Arnaiz, who has been the graphic eye of my business and a consistent cheerleader for my company (originally Foxfire Consulting) from the start. Thanks to expert photographer Elizabeth Linares, who uses photography as a spiritual practice and amazed me with the photos she's taken that are in my home, website and book.

Finally I thank my clients, students and friends. Your willingness to work and change your life for the better pushed me to find new, better and more effective ways to help you and thus enhanced my own life. It is a pleasure and an honor to be a part of your growth. I sincerely thank you for allowing me to be a part of your journey.

I love you all...

Why I Wrote This Book

SOMETIMES YOU JUST feel like you want to slap somebody. Anybody. I'm not a violent person, but frustration, anger and constantly feeling thwarted can make me want to lash out. I should say it used to. Now I know how to choose love even in the most difficult situations. Does that mean I make the loving choice every time? No. But I am *aware I have the choice* and do choose love much more than I used to! When I do choose love over fear, anger and frustration, my life is happier and more fulfilling, and I truly can live my joy, share my passion and love my life.

My dad and I always had a special connection. I was the firstborn and the most like him. I look like him, have similar mannerisms and most important, we both love the business process, especially the "art of the deal." At a very young age, we'd discuss how to maximize my babysitting income and grow my customer base. I loved learning from him. Witnessing his agonizing decline the last 20 months of his life was nothing short of torture for me and my family. My husband, sister, brother, sister-in-law, and our children were all affected by the long ordeal.

I had been researching and writing a business book for holistic healers when my dad suffered what turned out to be the first of many "significant medical events" in those last months. It was March 2012 and none of us - Dad, me, my family or our medical team - had any idea of the rollercoaster series of events that would unfold in the months that followed.

Going through that situation - coordinating information with our family as well as his network of friends, working with the hospital, doctors, staff, paid caregivers, medical offices, transportation services, insurance agencies, rehab facility, assisted living home and finally the hospice team - changed the way I look at the world. The constantly changing direction of his care in response to his volatile physical condition was beyond exhausting. And often it just didn't make sense.

I just wanted to slap somebody. Anybody would do! When my dad was moved into an assisted living facility after an extended stay in a nursing home, for example, we explained he was unusually restless during the night.

We explained we'd used a bedrail at home to prevent falls and asked to bring one in. Since a bedrail is considered a "restraint," it was prohibited in this licensed facility. I understand rules and that they have a purpose and probably have helped many patients. I certainly don't want any vulnerable person restrained or put in danger. But that's my common sense talking. The facility did give Dad a special bed that was lower to the floor, which was fine for a few days. Within his first week, he fell out of bed and broke his hip, requiring surgery and yet another lengthy stay in a physical rehab facility. Yeah, I wanted to slap somebody.

I was forced to examine my life and the ways I react to constant and ongoing stress in an effort to survive the ordeal myself. I slowly went from bitching about the situation, feeling sorry for myself and scared for my dad to lovingly accepting each event as it unfolded. I went from wanting to occasionally "do bodily harm" to medical personnel to understanding that these people were doing their best to help Dad while trying to balance hospital policy, federal mandates, insurance regulations and family requests with his personal care.

This book is the result of my years of spiritual training, study and work put to the test in this extreme situation. I figured out what worked and what didn't. I found the behaviors and thought patterns that enabled me to flow with this situation in a way that truly allowed me to be present for my dad and family while we lived through the uncertainty of each day. I went from wanting to slap somebody in frustration to trusting all was unfolding at the perfect pace. Although I eventually found peace in the later months, I did lapse into frustration at times.

It was a process. I was a mess on any given day that we received "bad" news about Dad's condition. Now I understand news isn't bad or good. It's just information. At a soul level Dad was always in control of his journey, and when I quit trying to manage his outcomes and simply did all I could to see he was safe and cared for, my experience of the drama lessened.

Watching someone you love slowly deteriorate in mind and body is a challenging experience for anyone to endure. It opens new doors and closes others. It changes you.

This situation definitely changed me and my family. I realize now it was for the better. This book is a direct result of the methods and techniques I used to weather months of stress and grief. It's how I was able to stop stressing and start loving my way through this difficult situation.

This Book is for You!

I KNOW YOU picked up this book because you thought it would be good for your spouse, your sister, the whiny guy at work - everyone in your life who's currently spouting anger, screaming with frustration and threatening to lash out. Guess what? It's for you. Really. No kidding. And I know because I was in the same place. I was perpetually upset and angry at life.

Yep. That was me, complaining about everything and everybody in the privacy of my own mind. The company I worked for was clueless, the neighbors were too nosey, my then husband seemed possessed, the weather sucked and don't get me started on the government! And I was my own worst critic. I was overweight, overworked and overwhelmed, and I easily made a list of all my faults, seemingly content to spiral further into my own hell. I believed I was a lousy wife, a bad mom and just too stupid to keep my body healthy. I felt like I was a useless human being who was living a life of pain, drowning in constant sadness. I had all the makings of a crappy life but a potentially catchy country music song. Too bad I can't sing.

At the time, I believed that my complaining was a way to relieve stress. Sort of an "explode or implode" method I suppose, which was an utter failure. I eventually began to understand that the more I complained to myself or others, the worse I felt. Instead of relieving my stress, the sense of doom only grew greater. It's this time in my life that I refer to as my "psycho mom" period. Don't believe me? Ask my kids.

I realize now that I must have spent hours every day - literally thousands upon thousands of thoughts - reviewing my life circumstances and judging them as horrible, bad, bleak, eventually thinking I was condemned to a sad life for no good reason I could fathom. I was really good at hiding this though. I went to church, prayed, read self-help books, watched Oprah, went to a therapist and took vitamins. If I thought it would help, I did it, took it, read it or watched it.

While I would have temporary reprieves, nothing seemed to help long term. I just kept driving myself into deep depression and potentially serious health issues.

Then I had a remarkable breakthrough. I could change my life...*I could change my life anytime I chose to.* What? No restraints were keeping me on this path of certain destruction except those created in my own mind. I could change *everything* with the power of my mind. Thus began my journey of self-discovery, which allowed me to collect the tools and techniques I use in my life and my coaching practice today. Some of my favorite tools came back to me and became my lifeline to love as I struggled with my dad's long decline. They enabled me to choose love when life seemed to hand me harsh circumstances. I found that choosing love always allowed me to handle any situation better.

This was my story but it could easily be yours. Our specific situations may be different, but you know what it feels like to be frustrated, upset and angry. You probably remember feeling situations in your life that were out of control. Love changes your perspective and your life experience.

I encourage you to read this book with an open mind and consider each principle and technique as presented. I've included examples of how my clients, students and friends have used them, so you can easily see how the methods were employed in typical daily situations. These techniques work if you use them consistently.

Can these techniques really take you from deep frustration to a place of peace and happiness? Yes. Is it magic? More a like miracle. The miracle of love.

Chapter 1

MEDITATE!

WHAT IF THERE was something that could help you choose love when you're frustrated? Help you lose weight? Soothe relationships? Improve your health? Transform you into a money magnet? *And it's free?*

That magic something is meditation.

Want to be happy? Meditate. Overweight? Meditate. Problem in your marriage? Meditate. Health issues? Meditate. Never have enough money? Meditate. Stressed out by your crazy family? Definitely meditate!

Years ago I offered a workshop entitled *"Meditation to Look Younger, Feel Thinner, Be Richer and Less Stressed!"* Meditation does all this and more. It's the secret to accessing your internal - and eternal - connection to Divine Spirit.

Many people are confused about what mediation is and how to do it. Because meditation is free, people often fail to see its value. How sad. Of all the spiritual books I've read, workshops I've attended, energy sessions I've received and given, nothing I've found produced more lasting and significant results than consistent meditation. I'm not an authority on meditation. I just know it works.

When I first learned to meditate, I was a full-time working mother, getting my MBA in night school and caring for chronically ill parents. I didn't have a lot of extra time and usually felt overwhelmed, exhausted and was constantly sick. Once I committed to a consistent meditation practice, I was more productive, found it easier to sleep and felt emotionally and physically strong. Over a short period of time, meditation moved me from frustrated to relaxed, upset to calm, and hopeless to hopeful. Meditation made the difference.

So what is meditation? It's a process of consciously relaxing your mind to transcend the never-ending flow of thoughts. Think of it as a conscious way to detach from your constant mind chatter into a mindful place of peace. It may take you a few tries to get the hang of this, but I guarantee there is nothing I've found that will make positive changes in your life faster than a consistent meditation practice. Nothing.

Why meditate? Countless medical, scientific and spiritual sources tout the benefits of consistent meditation. A few common benefits widely reported by people who consistently meditate include:

- Feeling happier and more at peace
- Increased social skills and feeling of "connectedness"
- Reduction or elimination of "stress eating" thus leading to lower weight
- Calmer thought patterns which can reduce "impulse buying" issues
- Lowered blood pressure and heart rate
- More relaxed muscles (some say they even appear younger once meditation drains stress from the face!)

- Increased brain function with improved memory and greater clarity
- Improved creativity and problem solving
- Greater pain tolerance
- Reduced overall stress (and reaction to specific stress triggers)

The most important benefit to those wishing to live a life of love is that of feeling connected to God, Source and the Universal Life-force Energy. No matter what name you identify with, the result is you feel a part of "the energy that runs through all things." You realize you're part of the pulse of the Universe as you go about your day, contributing your unique vibration to that of the whole. You're connected to the mighty oak tree and the smallest flower, connected to the quiet mountain stream as well as the roaring ocean, connected to the homeless man in your town and to your country's highest political leader. We're all one through the Divine Spark that burns within each one of us. Meditation makes this clear. It's much harder to criticize someone or something which you feel deeply connected to. And it's much easier to recognize the bonds that unite you.

A consistent meditation practice not only makes you aware of this Divine Spark but quiets the mind enough for you to actually hear the Divine guidance offered to you. In most Western cultures, the ego is so noisy that people never hear - or choose to ignore, or even worse, doubt - the whispers of Truth that are presented each and every moment. Meditation helps access that information to use in everyday decisions and allows you to develop and trust your innate intuitive abilities. The little voice within that has all the answers is suddenly available and easier to discern.

Let's be clear. A consistent meditation practice certainly doesn't mean you avoid problems or life challenges. But it does help you weather those issues with more grace and ease than ever before. You still make mistakes. Meditation gives you the rudder to right your actions more quickly, however, and get back on the path you truly want to explore. It'll help eliminate a good portion of the "noise" around you that comes in the form of gossip, fear and anger. You'll be better equipped to deal with those as well.

I've found that some of my coaching clients failed at meditation either because they used a technique that was uncomfortable for them or they just didn't understand how to begin or sustain a daily practice. Every client who faithfully meditated every day, even for as little as five minutes, achieved positive results.

I know what you're thinking. "I don't have time to meditate." "I tried it once and still felt crappy." "I can't sit in a position like a pretzel and chant." "What will my friends and family think?" Let's address those barriers one by one.

"I don't have time to meditate." I've heard meditation experts state that beginning with as little as five minutes a day, consistent meditators can quickly achieve positive results. Now come on - you don't have *five minutes a day?* How much time a day do you typically spend complaining or thinking negative thoughts? Use that time to meditate.

"I tried it once and still felt crappy." You once tried to walk and fell down, but you got back up and eventually learned to walk. Perhaps after several failed attempts you learned to ride a bike. You probably weren't a great driver at first, or a good cook or efficient at using your computer programs - it all took practice. So does meditation. Committing to a regular consistent practice of meditation is what yields the results you want.

"I can't sit in a position like a pretzel and chant." Luckily this is not required. There are many simple ways to comfortably meditate and I'll list a few techniques later in this chapter.

"What will my friends and family think?" They'll probably think you're calmer, happier and seem healthier and more fun to be around. And they'll probably want to know what you're doing so they can do it too!

Like everything else in life that's beneficial, you have to decide you want the desired benefit to wholeheartedly commit to the practice. So do you want to look younger, feel thinner, be richer and less stressed? Do you want to know how to choose love in even the most frustrating situations? Meditate!

How to Start

I meditate for **20** minutes soon after rising each morning before breakfast and again around 5:00p.m. if my schedule allows that day. I never miss my morning meditation and get in another session whenever possible. I'm consistent, and that's why it works to keep me grounded and centered. I strongly suggest you begin in the morning, but if that doesn't work for you, it's recommended that you time your meditation between meals.

There are various types of meditation and many start the same way. I'll describe that first and then discuss a few specific techniques. The meditation methods I've used most consistently are concentration, mindfulness and silent prayer. Read the description for each before you begin.

Start your meditation by finding a quiet place where you'll be undisturbed and turn off all phones and any other potentially noisy devices. Set a timer to monitor the length of your meditation session (start with at least five minutes once a day and work your way up to at least 20 minutes twice daily if that feels right for you).

Sit comfortably in a chair, feet flat on the ground, eyes shut, hands resting comfortably in your lap ideally with your palms up. The most important thing is to be comfortable. Take a few deep belly breaths and let it out slowly. (To take a "belly breath" place your hand right below your belly button and breathe deeply...your hand should be pushed out by your breath. If not, your breathing may be too shallow and only from the top of your lungs which limits your oxygen supply.) Now imagine you have "roots" coming out of the bottom of your feet and imagine pushing those roots down deep into the center of the earth, which will ground you. When you're ready to meditate, close your eyes and gently gaze towards your "third eye" area between your eyebrows which will help pop you into a theta brainwave that aids in a productive session. Decide on the technique you'd like to use and you're ready to begin.

Concentration

This is a favorite technique of many of my clients and students. In this method you simply stem the flow of thoughts by concentrating on an object outside yourself. It's that easy.

Many new meditators find success by using recorded guided meditation CDs or audio downloads that are available from any major bookstore as well as most metaphysical outlets, online sources and public libraries. This is a great way to start your meditation practice. You simply prepare yourself to meditate as described above, close your eyes and follow the voice of the narrator. Many guided meditations are designed around themes like abundance, stress relief or improved health. Choose your topic, choose your narrator and get started.

You can also concentrate on a single outside occurrence to get into a meditative state. For example, you can center yourself and begin to count each breath in, one, and out, two; in, three, out, four and so on. You can continue to count in order or cycle every 10 or 20 counts. Some people choose to breathe and concentrate on a specific phrase or mantra such as *"I am always connected to the Divine within," "Love flows to me and through me now"* or *"My world is filled with Divine Love."* Still others prefer to focus on an object like the sound of a tabletop water fountain, even a dripping faucet. With your eyes open you can softly focus on a flickering candle or fireplace flame as you relax. You can even do a "walking meditation" by totally concentrating on each step as you take a peaceful walk in nature. The technique works because you're giving your brain something to do instead of vainly trying to clear your mind of all thoughts.

This simple technique has proved effective for many of my clients. After one week, one woman became noticeably calmer and virtually stopped vicious shouting matches with her teenaged son. She felt so grounded and balanced that they were able to resolve differences that had been a problem for over a year. Another client found meditation helped his constant stress dissolve. He soon felt physically healthier and even had more success in his business.

Practicing Mindfulness

This meditation practice describes how to be mindful of "the now" and was made popular by Jon Kabat-Zinn. I've personally found it to be effective in alleviating mild to moderate pain. In this technique, you'll be concentrating about 25% on your breathing and 75% on the present moment. Here you simply breathe and observe what you're experiencing through your senses in the present moment without judgment from a detached state. It's easier than it sounds.

Let me explain.

When using this method, center yourself as described earlier, then with your eyes shut observe what your senses are experiencing right now. I usually begin at my feet and notice how they feel resting on the floor then work my way up the body. I notice how my clothes drape around me, notice the weight of my body as it rests in the chair, and how my hands are laying in my lap, all without allowing my mind to judge any of it.

I may notice my pants are fitting tightly because I feel a slight tension on the fabric around my middle but I do so without saying "I'm so fat!" See how it works? "I'm so fat!" is a judgment. Simply notice the feeling of the tight fabric and move on. Notice any sounds without judgment. Hear the neighbor's barking dog (without mentally adding "shut up!") Notice any smells that surround you without deciding they are "good" smells or "bad" ones. They're just scents.

The key in this method is to resist nothing. Your job in this meditation technique is to simply observe. If you feel pain anywhere, instead of cursing your luck and trying to resist it, note where the pain starts, the intensity and how it feels. Does it throb? Is it a dull pain? Sharp? Note all without judging that it's unfair to be in pain in the first place! By observing the pain in this way, you'll find you're soon either totally out of pain or that it's greatly reduced.

I've found the mindfulness technique very effective when I'm feeling particularly agitated or distracted. And just like with anything else in life, sometimes I want a change in my routine and rotate from my typical method to this one.

Centering Prayer

The first way I consciously meditated was by using the centering prayer method introduced by my pastor after he began studying the books of Father Thomas Keating. Keating rediscovered this forgotten Catholic practice in the 1970's and describes it as a way to experience God's presence within each of us. Centering prayer is a silent prayer method. Here's how it works.

Start by selecting a sacred word that symbolizes your intent to invite God's presence and action into your consciousness (I like to use "peace," "love," "Spirit," "welcome"). Center yourself with a few deep breaths and begin "to invite in the silence" by saying your sacred word to yourself as you let any thoughts that arise gently flow out of your consciousness like "a leaf gently floating on a river." As you sit, use the sacred word to bring back your intention when your thoughts become too distracting. Keating recommends meditating this way for 20 minutes twice daily. During church services, my pastor would ask the congregation to "imagine climbing into the lap of God, and rest there as a small child sits nestled in the lap of his father." I found this a very loving and effective way to connect with the Divine within.

I had the pleasure of attending a Centering Prayer workshop presented by Thomas Keating and can personally attest to his charismatic nature and passion for assisting others in rekindling their connection to God. This is an amazing technique, and I attribute my daily practice of this meditation to first giving me the inner strength I needed to make lasting positive changes in my life.

You probably have an idea which method appeals to you right now. So let's review:

1) Choose the meditation technique you feel most drawn to.

2) Make sure you choose a time to meditate before meals or at least two hours after eating.

3) If you want, set a timer to control the length of your session.

4) Sit comfortably in a chair, feet flat on the ground, eyes shut.

5) Take a few deep belly breaths and let them out slowly.

6) Imagine you have "roots" coming out of the bottom of your feet, and push them down into the center of the earth to ground you.

7) Begin using your method of choice.

Work with your preferred method for at least a week before trying an alternative method. Remember even five minutes a day makes a difference! Start with small sessions and work up to longer ones. Meditation is a wonderful way to allow yourself to begin to feel your connection to the Divine and "ignite the spark within." And it's an essential tool that allows you to choose love in any circumstance.

Chapter 2

THE POWER OF GRATITUDE

AN ATTITUDE OF sincere gratitude absolutely opens me up to love, and the reason is simple. *When your heart is filled with gratitude, there isn't room for anything less than love.* No room for anger, frustration or resentment. No room for guilt, regret or pain. Just love, gratitude and genuine appreciation. Gratitude opens you to peace, joy and even more to be truly grateful for. Gratitude helps you choose love.

Like any other practice, your "gratitude muscle" needs to be exercised, and it'll develop over time until it's just a way of life for you. What would your life look like if you felt deeply grateful for the world you live in? If you truly loved your body, your job and your home? If despite your differences, you were grateful for your friends, partner and the members of your family? Yes, even the ones that drive you crazy.

Living from a grateful space changes your perspective on everything and everyone. It's a way to easily welcome love into every aspect of your life. My family and I spent countless hours waiting outside the emergency room, surgery suite, hospital room, rehab facility and physician offices during the last 20 months of my dad's life. I found hundreds of things to resent during those hours and realized what those thoughts were doing to my mental and physical health. Unhealthy thoughts create an unhealthy body, and mine started to suffer. I often bragged I hadn't been sick in over eight years (not even a cold), but during this time I was forced to be on antibiotics three times for strep and laryngitis. A consistent gratitude practice helped turn this around.

Remembering that I felt blessed to be in my 50s and still have my dad warmed my heart. I started to find things to feel grateful for during those long days in various medical settings and found everything started to shift. While I couldn't in good conscience feel grateful that I was spending yet another day in the hospital with Dad, I was truly grateful for the time my brother Bill, sister Kathy and I spent together. We have our own families, and it's rare just the three of us are together to discuss our lives and our shared past. Hours waiting for a lab result or for a specific physician to see Dad gave us time to reminisce, talk about our future and get silly. My brother can get very silly. We laughed a lot. My sister becomes more of the "Momma Bear" in these situations, ready to do battle with *anyone* who messes with her family. I'm thankful for my siblings even if this wasn't the situation I would have chosen to gain that insight.

I also found it gratifying to work with my brother and sister, cleaning out and selling my parents' home. We spent over 25 Christmas mornings there while Granddaddy and Grandmommy watched our children grow. Our family memories were there in that house. And now it was time to go through my parents' belongings, put everything in piles and "dispose" of it. Again, gratitude was my saving grace. Working with my brother and sister, we revisited our childhood and our children's as we packed the Sippy cups they had used and lovingly donated the platter that for decades had displayed our family turkey each Thanksgiving. I felt the gratitude swell inside as I revisited precious times in my past, so thankful of the specific cast of characters I call my family.

I do want to give a disclaimer. We're not the "Leave It to Beaver" family I saw on television growing up. We fought, we had our issues and we handled many of them poorly. In hindsight, I'm truly grateful for each opportunity this group gave me to learn and grow even when the growth was painful. Looking at my past through a filter of gratitude unearthed many truths I had never before seen about myself and my personality. I'm thankful for that.

As I became increasingly aware of the power of this emotion, I added periodic gratitude classes to my coaching practice. Each workshop had an opportunity for the students to discuss what they were profoundly grateful for and the discussions were always eye-opening. After people listed God, family, friends, job, etc. - the expected list - the dialogue got interesting.

"What else are you truly thankful for?" I asked one evening. "Maybe something that surprised you?" One of my regulars raised her hand and replied, "I'm very grateful for my fingernails."

"Your *fingernails?*" I asked, not sure I had heard correctly.

"Yes!" she answered. "I realized that I need my fingernails to peel labels and attach them to files. I do it all day long. If I didn't have fingernails I couldn't do my job as quickly or efficiently as I do. I never realized until now how important all my parts are!" Nothing is too insignificant to be grateful for.

One student mentioned being grateful for his determination to stick to an exercise program, resulting in a more flexible body. Another was thankful for a power outage that turned off the television and prompted her to pick up a book that changed her life. One woman voiced appreciation for forgetting to pack her makeup on a recent trip. She said she felt free and natural for the first time in years! Another was thankful for a broken computer since she found the love of her life behind the counter of the repair shop. Look back on your life while you focus on gratitude and see what you notice. Gratitude helps you rediscover the many gifts that have been presented to you.

I found there are many ways to make a gratitude practice part of daily life and I've listed a few of my favorites below. While all these can be done individually, they're fun to discuss with family or friends. The key is to truly feel the energy of gratitude as you do these. No need to force yourself to feel grateful for something you're not. Cultivating the feeling of gratitude is the goal here as you discover what you have to be thankful for, even in unlikely circumstances. Staying in "an attitude of gratitude" is what opens you to love and even more to be grateful for.

Gratitude Exercises

Say Thank You And Mean It: I bet you're great at saying "thank you" many times a day, but how many times do you mean it? Each time you utter "thank you," take an extra minute to acknowledge why you're thankful - out loud or silently as you deem appropriate - and feel the energy of sincere gratitude warm your heart. When faced with harsh situations or events, look for people or things to be grateful for. While my dad was undergoing painful medical treatment, I was aware of the lovely lady who came to clean his hospital room every day. She always spoke to each of us, asked permission before she "tidied up" and took time to speak encouraging words to Dad. She truly was a ray of sunshine in what became a string of dreary days. I was grateful for her cheerful attitude and thanked her profusely.

Keep a Gratitude Journal: I've had a Gratitude Journal for years and it's taken many forms. Sometimes I simply list three to five things that happened that I was grateful for at the end of each day. Other times I began the day with a of list five things I was grateful for from the previous 24 hours and added three things I wanted to be grateful for in the next 24. I've often helped my clients and students begin a Gratitude Journal by giving them a few topics to consider. In these exercises they're asked to create a list and note why they're grateful for each entry.

Practice completing the following sentences with at least 10 items, followed by the reason you're grateful for each.

I am truly grateful for my relationship with…
I am so grateful for these life experiences…
I am thankful for these aspects of my physical body…
I am truly grateful and admire these traits/skills/talents of mine…
I am so thankful for these people in my life…
I am truly grateful for these things I have in my life…

A Helping of Gratitude at Dinner: I grew up reciting a blessing before dinner, but as a kid I don't remember it really meaning anything much except the mashed potatoes were on the way. We went around the Thanksgiving table and named something we were grateful for, which usually required me to begin thinking several days in advance for a gratitude that would impress my family. It should be easier. I've come up with a gratitude exercise that's easy, spontaneous and heartfelt that can be used by individuals or families who want to cultivate an attitude of gratitude.

On a sheet of paper create a series of open-ended sentences with at least 20 categories of things/people/places/events you (or any family member or guest) could be grateful for. Cut these up into slips and put them in an attractive container on your table. Before the meal, have everyone choose a slip, and go around the table encouraging everyone to finish their sentence stating what they're grateful for and why. Your sentences could include phrases like:

I am so grateful I learned _____ *because*_____.

I'm thankful for my friend _____ *because*_____.

I'm happy and grateful I'm living in _____
  *because*_____.

*I'm thankful for (name a specific person like Mom/Dad/
  Sis or anyone special to you) because*_____.

*I'm thankful I have (name a household convenience like
  running water, soap, electricity, etc.) because*_____.

*I'm grateful for (event like Mother's Day, Sunday football,
  an upcoming party) because*_____.

You get the idea. This is a great way to introduce children or the "whiner" in your life to a new way of thinking. Yes, you'll get some resistance and "funny" answers occasionally, but often a game like this opens you up energetically and expands your opportunities to be grateful.

List 100 Gratitudes: In his book *Be Happy,* Dr. Robert Holden describes this gratitude exercise as a way to consciously connect to Spirit, increase your well-being and become more heart-centered. I found it did all this and much more. In this assignment, Robert encourages you to list 100 things you're truly grateful for, noting not only the "what" but the "why." When I offer this to my clients, I tell them to approach this exercise from a calm and centered space. Carve out some time and take a few deep breaths before you begin.

At each sitting, you need write only 10 to 15, so the entire list may take a few days or a week to complete. Just begin and keep going until you've listed at least 100. I encourage my clients to create their list in any way that feels right for them. Some people like to list whatever comes to them each day. Some prefer to create categories like childhood, family, work, physical body, experiences, life events, things, etc. I've found the most profound insights from compiling your list in chronological order.

It's interesting to look for gratitude in your history. For example, many Baby Boomers and members of the Sandwich Generation (people responsible for aging parents and children at the same time) might be thankful to have been experienced a world before cell phones and computers were common in most households. While most enjoy modern technology, many feel grateful to have developed specific skillsets thanks to a culture that didn't have those conveniences when they were children. They learned to play outside. They know how to converse. They remember experiencing the shock of seeing President Kennedy shot, the Civil Rights Movement unfold, an American first walk on the moon. This generation is often grateful to have lived through these events instead of learning about them in school. Some can easily remember having only three television channels. *Yes, I said only three television channels.* And when television was still a new technology, those three channels provided much to be grateful for. Everyone watched movies like *It's a Wonderful Life*, *A Charlie Brown Christmas* and *The Wizard of Oz* on the same day and time. It was a shared cultural experience and one that was savored.

I first decided to create my list by decade, beginning from birth through age 10. This seemed simple enough until I started. Once I began, I actually realized there were many pre-birth conditions I was extremely grateful for. I'm grateful I was born in the United States. I'm very grateful to be born in a small town in Virginia, nestled at the foothills of the Blue Ridge Mountains but less than 50 miles from Washington, DC. Even though it's more physical maintenance, I'm thankful to be born a female. See what I mean?

As I began to tackle what I was truly grateful for through my tenth birthday, I was flooded with memories of childhood friends, special visits with my Minnesota and Nebraska relatives, even the smell of my Grandmother Haworth's banana nut bread fresh from the oven.

Remembering the bread sparked another memory. I was instantly transported back to 1968 in Lexington, Nebraska, spending time with Grandma in the kitchen, just the two of us, my 11-year-old frame hunched over her table as I diligently recorded the recipe and waited for the bread to come out of the oven. This triggered more sleeping memories to emerge from my unconscious about my Westcott relatives and the gift of special time with them.

During the *100 Gratitudes* exercise, I was at times overcome, remembering a kind gesture that years later brought grateful tears to my eyes. As you can imagine, I was never able to list only 10 to 15 gratitudes per decade. High school and college accounted for at least 30! You'll find this exercise sparks memories lying dormant in your unconscious unveiling layers of even deeper gratitudes for you to relish and enjoy.

I encourage you to create and keep adding to your list as the grateful memories continue to flood in, always following the "what" with the "why." The beauty of this exercise occurs when you allow yourself to stay in the flow of gratitude and recognize the special life you've led. You may find as I did, while your life didn't unfold the way you envisioned as a child, it's been the perfect path for you. From an energetic perspective, since "like attracts like," the more thankful your attitude, the more you will bring things into your life to be grateful for.

Giving More than Gratitude

Another way to demonstrate a grateful heart to the Universe is to donate your time, money and skills to causes you believe in. This beautifully compliments your gratitude by sharing your energy while you give others the opportunity to be grateful. Donate money to support organizations that do work you believe in and make sure every dollar is donated with a grateful heart.

Volunteer when you feel called to do so, and be grateful not only for the cause you're supporting but for your skills that can be of service. The energy at a well-run event that uses volunteers is amazing and spreads love to all involved.

Compliments, heartfelt thank-you notes, homemade gifts, a good joke or a beautiful smile are other things that can be "donated" and are more appreciated than you know. I've had clients in crisis tell me how much they appreciated receiving cards, food and flowers in response to a tragedy. Phone calls, emails and visits "just to check on you" were also listed as ways people felt valued and remembered.

Monetary donations, volunteering time and thoughtful gestures are all great ways to demonstrate gratitude and circulate love in the world.

I believe an "attitude of gratitude" is an essential ingredient for a happy, healthy, fulfilling life. Choosing gratitude is a way to open your heart and allow you to choose love more easily. *When your heart is truly filled with gratitude, there isn't room for anything less than love.* Gratitude opens you to peace, joy and even more to be grateful for. Gratitude helps you choose love.

Chapter 3

YOU ARE WHAT YOU THINK

C ONSIDER THIS BUDDHA quote: *"We are what we think. All that we are arises with our thoughts. With our thoughts, we make the world."* You are what you think. If you think your day will be a disaster, a disaster it is. If you think your day will be a happy one, you'll be right again. Industrialist Henry Ford said it this way, *"Whether you think you can, or you think you can't - you're right."* According to philosopher Soren Kierkegaard, *"Our life always expresses the result of our dominant thoughts."*

So if you think you're a failure, you will live that truth. If you think you're a kind person, you'll demonstrate kindness. Are we doomed by our thoughts? Not at all. Norman Vincent Peale said, *"Change your thoughts and you change your world."* Award-winning singer/songwriter Willie Nelson is quoted as saying, *"Once you replace negative thoughts with positive ones, you'll start having positive results."* Willie gets it. All these people understood the power of the mind to create reality. And they understood everyone has the power to change their reality by changing their thoughts.

I know, I know - you've heard about the power of changing your thoughts to change your life and have probably read books demonstrating how to consciously create your life with your thoughts. And you believe some of it. I believe all of it. I've seen countless times how the energy of my thoughts not only crafted my life experience, but absolutely affected those around me.

Several years ago I was learning to scuba dive in the Bahamas. On the second day out with my instructor, I was still awestruck by the beauty at the bottom of the ocean. The coral, the spectacular array of sea creatures, and the vastness of the sea - it was just incredible. And I could see it all because I was *breathing* under water! It was unbelievable. I remembered my television hero, Jacques Cousteau, and could hear his powerful voice in my head, eloquently describing in his beautiful French accent the breathtaking underwater scene that enveloped me.

We were diving near a large coral reef when a school of brightly colored fish silently glided by followed by a trio of six-to-eight-foot-long reef sharks. I watched with amazement and noted the group was only about 10 feet away from me. *What? The sharks were only 10 feet away from ME!* In a flash, the theme from *Jaws* started playing in my head, as did each brutal bloody scene from every single shark movie I've ever seen. And I've seen *a lot*. The tempo of the song increased, and as I became completely terrified, one shark broke away from the group and began circling me. I could see the shark's dead eyes staring through me and I became even more horrified. Quint's famous line in *Jaws* flooded back to me, *"You know the thing about a shark, he's got... lifeless eyes, black eyes, like a doll's eye."* It's true.

As the shark got closer and closer, I was forced to drop down on my belly between two coral shelves, where

I was trapped. I was breathing hard and using up oxygen fast when I realized there was at least 50 feet of ocean straight up between me and the boat. The more scared I became, the more aggressive the shark got. I remembered hearing that sharks could sense fear and were drawn to any creature that gave off "victim" vibes. Even in full panic, a small voice inside me realized *I have to calm down*. I forced myself to breathe deep and slow. I began to repeat "I am safe, I am safe, I am safe" over and over in my mind. As I felt my body start to relax, the shark began to lose interest, and as I completely relaxed into the calm, it turned and swam away. The only thing that changed in this scenario was my thought pattern. You think I believe our thoughts matter? You bet I do!

Need more reasons to consciously change your thoughts? Here's a good one. Your unconscious doesn't recognize the difference between what you perceive as real and what you've imagined. That's exactly why my heart starts to race and I become frightened when I'm safe and sound sitting on my couch watching scary shark movies. I live in the foothills of the Blue Ridge Mountains a few hours away from the nearest beach, and not even the Syfy Channel has spotted flying mountain sharks yet. Even when *I know I'm physically safe*, my body still reacts to what I see on the television screen, which causes my physical stress response. This is why I became frightened diving in the Bahamas. My mind remembered the shark movies, and my body reacted to what it perceived as danger even though the sharks I saw were just swimming by me. At least they were in the beginning, before I became afraid and my body reacted as a potential "victim." My panic was caused by my thoughts, not in response to what the sharks were actually doing.

Your body reacts to what the mind perceives. That's why you cry at sad movies even when you know it's a work of fiction. Your body will often tense when you read about a dangerous situation that's occurred thousands of miles away. Ever wake up from a vivid dream in a full sweat? Your body is reacting to the details of the dream. It doesn't recognize your physical body was actually lying down asleep during the dream. Feed your body scary, angry thoughts, and you and your body perceive a scary, angry world. Want to see more love in the world? Think more loving thoughts. Your body will react accordingly and relax.

No one needs more stress. Chronic stress has been shown to make us physically weaker, temporarily lower our IQ and create a host of physical issues. Who needs that? You can learn to control your thoughts and it's the quickest way to change your experience of life events. Remember that "like begets like," so fearful, angry thoughts will create even more fearful, angry thoughts while joyful, happy thoughts will create more of those.

I've been very inspired reading the biographies of people I admire. I love seeing how their thoughts created lives no one believed were possible. I was a young girl watching *The Wonderful World of Disney* with my dad one Sunday evening when Walt himself told us about his plans for *Walt Disney World*, his new project to be built in Florida.

"He's nuts!" I remember my dad saying. "He can't build on swamp-land with a bunch of alligators." My dad was smart, but ol' Walt was brilliant and we all know what stands in Florida today. Disney World is the most visited attraction on the planet, and it all started as a crazy idea in Walt's head. *"If you can dream it, you can do it. Always remember this whole thing was started by a mouse,"* said Walt Disney. I love Oprah Winfrey's story as well.

Who in their right mind would have believed a poor little black girl born to a single teenage mother in rural Mississippi in the 1950s would become a billionaire and revered as the most influential woman in the world? Every one of Oprah's accomplishments started as a single thought in her own mind. Thoughts are powerful. Focused thoughts can be unstoppable.

The belief that thoughts create reality is not a "new age" idea. Buddha spoke of the power of thoughts nearly 500 years before Christ: *"The mind is everything. What you think you become."* In his play *Hamlet*, Will Shakespeare wrote, *"There is nothing either good or bad but thinking makes it so."* Ralph Waldo Emerson proves my earlier point when he stated, *"An action is the perfection and publication of thought."* Walt Disney published his thoughts at Walt Disney World. The belief that your thoughts create your reality has been around for centuries and is now even being explored in traditional medical settings. Want to change your thoughts? It's easier than you think.

How to Change Your Thoughts Now

In the middle of a crisis, irritation, frustration or *anytime* you feel uncomfortable, you can replace your thoughts and positively affect your mood and attitude. I'm not suggesting you ignore a potentially dangerous situation. I am suggesting that evaluating a situation from a calm emotional space can lead to better decisions!

"The quickest way to change your psychology is to change your physiology," is a favorite quote of mine I once heard by peak performance coach and self-help author Anthony Robbins. It works. When I find myself spiraling down into a well of negative thoughts, I immediately change my body position to break the thought pattern. If I'm sitting, I stand up. If I'm standing, I sit down. When that's not possible, I can always sit up straight, pull my shoulders back and breathe deeply. Smile, and if possible, look toward a natural light source and imagine feeling "recharged." Even changing where I sit can immediately change my perspective and help me feel more awake.

Several years ago, I was an adjunct professor at a large urban university where I taught a weekly three-hour class from 4:00 to 7:00p.m. one spring semester. After about 90 minutes, my students would get restless and sleepy. I feel certain this had nothing to do with my skill as a lecturer but on the time of day the class was scheduled. I would often have them stand up and stretch, but if I was about to discuss something complex midway through our time period, I would actually have them change seats. Everyone in the back row came to the front. If a student was seated on my left, he had to go sit on my extreme right. The result was always the same. The change in perspective immediately woke the students up and participation soared.

Other ways to quickly change your thoughts:

- Change your scenery; move into a different room, go for a ride or take a walk in nature and soak up the energy of the trees and natural environment. If you are stuck indoors, look at pictures of nature or watch a serene nature documentary.
- Engage with your pets; play with the cat, talk to your fish or play catch with the dog.
- Look at beautiful images; keep a book of varied landscapes from around the world, cute baby or animal pictures, lovely flowers, artwork or architectural marvels.
- Reread thank-you notes, love letters or any written words of appreciation and love that have been sent to you. (What? You don't keep these? Start your "Feel Good File" today!)
- Bring some of nature indoors; energize your space with flowers, plants and small trees.
- Focus on what you want to happen; use creative imagery to "see yourself" in a successful situation. Concentrate on developing a feeling of peace and calm by imagining what it would be like to already be there.
- Change your perspective by changing the furniture around or at least chair placement. Any room where you notice you experience the most negative thoughts could be changed. Shift furniture, change colors in the area or add plants. Consult a feng shui book or practitioner to help, but make the room visually different.

- Eat organic and healthy; only consume processed sugar, caffeine, alcohol and rich foods in moderation. I've found the healthier my diet, the healthier my thoughts!
- Play fun music and *move;* go ahead and dance and the more outrageous, the better. Make the movements *big* and feel the energy in your body change. Although my husband Joe is my favorite dance partner, my cat tolerates dancing with me when I need a quick change of attitude. She mostly watches, but that's a form of cat involvement as far as I'm concerned.
- Sing your favorite upbeat song and make it *loud;* this works nicely with dancing but is perfect when you're stuck in the car and need to release some energy.
- Connect with people or places that make you happy. Need to turn on the Comedy Channel? Call up your old roommate who always has a good joke? Does looking at your high school yearbook make you laugh? Do it.
- Say a heartfelt prayer.
- Meditate.
- Write in your gratitude journal.
- Alter negative thought patterns and energy blocks with massage, Reiki, reflexology, exercise or yoga.

It might seem overwhelming at first, but if you remember to implement even one or two of these suggestions, you'll quickly see a world of difference in your perspective.

Get the idea? Everyone has days where their mind wanders to the worst possible scenario, including life-threatening physical pain, tragic loss or invasion by a hostile alien civilization. If you're experiencing extreme grief or trauma, seek appropriate help. If you're a victim of your own pattern of negative thoughts, realize you have the power to change that and consciously make the change. A good coach, therapist or practitioner can help as well.

How to Change Your Thoughts Permanently

While I love the quick techniques for "emergency thought situations," a life of real peace and happiness comes from working to permanently change our thought patterns. Even then you'll have those days where you're tested, but with the tips above, you can easily change them. For long-term change, understand it's a process that will yield major results over time. The farmer doesn't plant his field and expect to harvest crops the next day. You too are planting seeds of change in your life that will sprout and grow in the perfect time.

Two major factors that aid in instilling a positive happy attitude have been discussed earlier in this book: consistent meditation and gratitude practices. Regularly applied over time, these two techniques will give you the ability to think through any situation with more grace and ease than you've probably ever experienced.

A third recommendation is to keep your body in good shape with proper diet and exercise. My girlfriend swears she has happier, more productive thoughts when she exercises and practices yoga. Since both have been found to effectively control stress, this makes perfect sense. She feels healthier, happier, looks great and has more energy, which helped her build a successful healing business. Before she started exercising, she'd often fall victim to thoughts of "I can't do this" or "I'm not good enough." Not anymore. Changing her thoughts and taking care of her physical body has changed her life for the better.

I've found that when I am properly hydrated with pure water, practice even minimal exercise and eat good quality protein with lots of green vegetables, I'm at my very best. My body feels great and my thinking is clear. I got the help of trained holistic health counselors to guide me and advise you to seek professional guidance in this area as well. Another way I've found vital in keeping my thoughts positive and on track is to create what I call a "Life Script."

The Importance of a Life Script

One important key to getting what you desire in life is *knowing what you want*. It's really that simple. You may tend to forget you're creating your life through focused thought and continue old patterns of concentrating on fears which perpetuate *more* fear and fearsome thoughts. So how do we keep positive focus on our desires? The best way I've found is by writing what I call a Life Script. This one technique will not only help you define what you want, but keep your thoughts and energies directed, allowing the Universe to bring to you what you desire. This is a fantastic way to create your life with your thoughts.

Why Write It Down?

Throughout the years I've studied books, recordings and techniques from many wonderful motivational teachers. Many of these teachers cite the importance of writing down your goals and note that the likelihood of reaching your goals actually increases with this practice. That's exactly what happened for me. Long before I knew much about energy techniques, I worked at a major university outside of Washington, DC, and desperately wanted to start my own coaching practice in my hometown of Warrenton, Virginia.

I created a document describing *exactly* what I wanted my life to look like. I described my marriage, where I lived, my business (including location, type of clients, desired income level and personal development goals), my donations to charity and volunteer work, my overall health and even the type of car I wanted to drive. I tried to think of everything that touched my existence in this physical life and wrote my Life Script in the positive, present tense as if I was already living the life I described. It felt great! Not only did I create my Life Script, I reread it daily for a few weeks, then weekly for a couple weeks, and then at least once a month to keep my goals uppermost in my mind. In less than a year, I had the office I imagined, the location I wanted and my dream car. It was incredible!

Did I get everything I wanted? No. It was then I really started to understand the importance of my beliefs in creating my experience. I also noticed that sometimes what I thought I wanted had shifted or morphed into something else over time. Those items and the ones I was unclear about were the ones that did not appear in my life within the first year. Coincidence? I think not.

Life Script Example

Confused about what a Life Script looks like? Here's a short example from a Reiki practitioner who nearly doubled her business in just three months after writing her comprehensive script. She described her desired life experience in three areas: business, home and personal.

MY LIFE

BUSINESS

I am a financially successful and respected business owner who is an instrument for Divine healing with Reiki and other complimentary modalities. I have at least five clients a day, three days a week and they experience true healing on physical, mental and spiritual levels. My clients are open to healing, appreciate my service, pay joyfully and on time. They come to me during the hours that suit me and my family the best. Many take Reiki classes from me. I teach all levels of Reiki to eager students who seek to help themselves and others heal. I teach through public institutions, my own private classes and for specific groups that include massage therapists, the clergy, mental health professionals, nurses and other health care workers. I teach at least two classes per month. My classes are always full with the perfect students for me. I am happy and know we help each other learn and grow.

I also teach and organize workshops for healers twice a year and offer personal coaching for alternative healers. I have a minimum of 10 coaching clients paying $400/month each and every month. My clients are motivated, appreciate my service, are eager and open to learn and pay joyfully for what they receive. I continue to personal coach via phone and do long distance healings when I travel.

I have a beautiful office in Richmond, Virginia, close to my home with separate rooms for treatment, business, storage, reception, teaching and meditation functions. Everyone who enters feels peace and healing in this space. They feel safe and welcome.

My business produces abundant financial rewards in addition to substantial joy and personal growth for my family and me. My income is at least $12,000 a month. My family and I share this financial abundance with charities that touch our hearts. Abundance freely flows to me and through me to others. I do 10% of my Reiki pro bono and take a number of personal coaching clients in exchange for a free-will donation to charity.

I am happy and fulfilled knowing I am helping others change their lives. I meet fascinating people from all over the world and am blessed to know them and their stories. I feel I am doing Divine work and am fulfilling my life purpose. My family is happy, healthy and totally supportive of my work. They assist me in the business. I have a successful fulfilling business and have all the time I want to be with my family and friends.

HOME LIFE

Our welcoming home is full of light, love and peace. We are happy and comfortable in it. We have a beautiful spacious log home with breathtaking views of the river. It is a beautiful place with beautiful energy. The house is an easy commute to my office and is in a peaceful area that is protected from becoming over-populated or overgrown. It is always protected and never suffers from damage of any kind, including weather, fire, earthquake, theft, etc.

The log house is big and open with ample room for all our family and friends to visit. There is a covered porch, open deck behind big windows and screened in porch so we can enjoy our views year round. We have at least four bedrooms and a place for my home office. My husband has a fantastic space for his office as well plus a garage. There is a fabulous master bedroom with a Jacuzzi and a hot tub on the deck. We have great kitchen and dining room areas for entertaining. Our house is full of love.

Taking care of the property and cleaning the house is never an issue. We attract exactly the people we need to do this for us and we bless their lives as they bless ours.

PERSONAL

I am a healthy, happy and toned size 10. I feel beautiful and love my body. My husband is an attentive, respectful, supportive and passionate husband and I am the same type of wife to him. We grow together and develop mentally, physically and spiritually. We laugh and enjoy life.

We have family and friends locally and throughout the world that connect and grow with us. We are a blessing to each other. We take at least two vacations each year anywhere we choose and always have the financial resources to enjoy our life and to share with others.

Why did this work for my client? She took the time to really think about what she wanted and wrote it down! This is just a quick example of what a Life Script can look like. You can add any details you want to create the life you want to lead.

The Importance of Feelings and Gratitude in Reading Your Life Script

Teachers like Wayne Dyer, Ester Hicks and Vianna Stibal say we need to know how it *feels* to have what we want or we simply won't recognize when our desires materialize. I agree! The clearer you get with what you want and the more you feel what it's like to experience what you desire, the quicker you manifest. Therefore, it's of the utmost importance to really stay in the place of feeling your desires as you read and re-read your Life Script. As you write and read your Life Script, imagine how you'll feel when what you describe is a physical reality *and feel truly grateful for it.* The more you can stay in the energy of that feeling of gratitude, the quicker your desires come into your life.

The beauty of this exercise is that you can - and should - update your life script when your needs change. Maybe you thought you'd always wanted a Prius and you put that in your Life Script - until you saw your best friend's new Mini-Cooper. Like it better? Ever considered a Lamborghini? Just edit your life script!

Be Clear About What You Want and Concentrate on the End Result

Be sure you are totally clear about what you want. For example, I used to say I had clients and I got them, but they never wanted to pay, many didn't want to try energy techniques and were late for appointments. Not my idea of my "ideal" clients. Now I have in my script: *"I attract* the perfect clients for me who appreciate my skills, are committed to healthy change and who pay joyfully, in full and on time." My clientele has changed dramatically as has the success of my business. Here's another wonderful benefit of having paying clients: I can gift others with sessions, donate to the charities I love *and* always pay my bills on time.

Another tip would be to *concentrate on the end result* of what you want in your Life Script. Forget how you'll get it. That will come in more wonderful ways than you could ever imagine if you just let it. *"I enjoy driving a beautiful new hunter green Mercedes convertible that is fully paid for"* is an example of concentrating on the end result. *"I win the lottery and am able to buy a beautiful new hunter green Mercedes convertible"* is concentrating on the *way* you acquire the car. That's a no-no. No need to instruct the Universe on how to bring your desires to you. Your job is to set your intentions, move forward with your plans and be open to receiving with gratitude.

Need another example of concentrating on the end result? Here's a line I love: *"I am a healthy, fit and toned size 10."* This concentrates the energy on the ultimate desire instead of the process as in the phrase *"I lose 20 pounds and go to the gym."* In the second example, the emphasis is on the future - *I lose 20 pounds*- instead of the current condition that is desire -*I am a healthy, fit and toned size 10.* See the difference? It's an important one. Keep your statements focused on the end result in positive, present tense sentences.

One more important tip: While you want to inject gratitude into what you desire to have, you want to always be grateful for what's currently in your life. The energy needs to stay positive all around. It's fine to write about a job you want to manifest by stating "I enjoy my new job at DLH Company" as long as you are still grateful for the job you currently have at the JLM Corporation. Avoid giving negative energy to the things you don't want in your life. That actually energizes them as well and keeps what you don't want in place. Focus on what you want, and trust all will manifest for your highest and best.

Ready to consistently change your thoughts about your life? Get writing!

Write Your Own Life Script

Create your own positive document written in the present tense and touch any category that affects your life such as: health, personal relationships, finances, spirituality, home, business/career, hobbies or any other area that feels right for you.

IMPORTANT POINT: This is *your* Life Script. You're using this manifesting technique to help you permanently change your thoughts and consciously create your life. You can manifest for yourself only. For example, you may write *"my family is financially stable with more than enough money flowing into our accounts every month."* This speaks to your financial experience which is appropriate. You cannot write, *"My husband/wife has a new job with The Empowered Spiritual Path company and is making over $100,000 a year that they choose to spend on me."* OK, you *could* write that but it probably won't work the way you'd like. You cannot manifest for someone else since that would be bypassing their free will. That's another no-no.

Write your script, detailing the life you want to live, then read it once a day, every day for 30 days, then once a week for a month, and once a month thereafter to keep the life you've created uppermost in your consciousness. Edit as your desires change. As you become more aware of what you're creating in your life, it's not unusual to "tweak" the script a bit or to outright change your mind about something. No worries! Make your edits, keep reading the script and watch the miracles come into your life! Why? Because you've changed your thoughts.

Get the idea? Now in your version, you'll expand on the type of home you'd like, noting the location and any details that are important such as closet space or a detached garage or pool. Remember to add the feeling you want to have in the text. Believe me, a *"warm, comfortable loving home"* is much more important that a *"colonial house with a traditional center hall."* Trust me. When you come from a loving attitude and release any attachment to the end result, you'll always love what you get anyway. Give love an open to door to show you the wonders of life.

Now use this chapter to get started and write your own Life Script. Change your thoughts, and see how you can create a life filled with love and happiness. It's much better than wanting to slap somebody!

Chapter 4

WHAT IF LIFE IS WORKING FOR YOU?

CONSIDER THIS: LIFE is working for me. *Life is working for me? Life is working for me and for my highest and best?* What a concept! Have you looked at my life? All the petty inconveniences of life like missing car keys, being late for work, only finding one sock, PC crashes - as well as the struggles, pain and loss - all working for my benefit? And the benefit of others? How could that be? As long as I was focused on the drama of the day, this certainly didn't seem possible. When I consciously choose love as my guide, however, it's an accepted - and expected - way of life. It took an interesting train of events to help me realize the truth of this statement. Here's how it happened.

I'd been contemplating this very principle and working to allow myself to truly believe whatever happened, appeared to happen, or looked like it might happen was all for my ultimate good. When discussing this with a few close friends, several had the same question: "Are you nuts?"

Regardless of my skeptical buddies, I was determined to explore the idea. I must admit it was much more of a challenge than I anticipated.

I'd been introduced to this theory several years ago in the writings of Louise Hay. I had just begun to discover metaphysical/spiritual literature then and was reading everything I could to understand how my actions and thoughts did indeed create my own experience. This little gem of wisdom must have slipped through the cracks, only to be reintroduced when I attended a five-day "Coaching Success" program with Dr. Robert Holden in New York.

In the safe but intense environment of Robert's workshop, we delved into the meaning of success, happiness and yes, the concept that "Life is working for me" and how shifting your belief to accept this can positively shift your experience of life. It was a busy, fun, and eye-opening five days. All this was well and good and totally believable as long as I was in the group environment with like-minded folks who were willing to give it a shot too. Then I went home.

I'll never forget the next several days - when I first realized *Life was working for me and for my highest and best*. Robert's program had ended on the Sunday evening before Thanksgiving, and I spent that evening relishing the new concepts I'd learned and how I'd incorporate them into my coaching practice. I boarded the train home on Monday, still full of excitement. The next two days were filled with clients as I played "catch up" in the office after being gone for a week.

In a moment of "Why'd I do that?" I suddenly realized on Wednesday that I had volunteered to bring a pumpkin pie to my brother's house, where my family would gather for our Thanksgiving feast the next day. Maybe I *was* nuts! I'd just come back from a week of training and was working long hours to see a week's worth of clients in two days. Now yes, I could have purchased a pumpkin pie from the grocery store, but I had gone into *great detail* with my family about the merits of *my* recipe and how we simply must have a homemade pie. My sister really should have stopped me but she didn't. Now I was fretting over the stupid pie, and anyone who understands the importance of a good pumpkin pie to the overall success of Thanksgiving knows this was close to a full-blown crisis.

Then I remembered.

What *if* Life was working for me? Yeah, I had momentarily forgotten my new mantra: *"Life is working for me!"* OK, it'll all work out I thought. I surrendered to this truth and decided I'd finish with my clients and proceed to the store. At that point, I'd assess how tired I was and either purchase a "store bought" pie or the ingredients to make one. I felt the stress leave my body.

Then it happened - my first miracle. One of my favorite clients came in for her session bearing a huge pumpkin pie made by our local five-star bakery. This was the same pie that had been awarded "Washington DC Area's Best Pumpkin Pie" only days before by a respected regional magazine. Oh yeah, crisis averted! While the irony and timing wasn't lost on me, I, being human, still needed a bit more convincing.

By Thanksgiving morning, I was in a panic as I prepared for what would be a new tradition for my family. Living in the memory support unit at a local assisted living facility, my dad was unable to travel even a short distance to be with the family for Thanksgiving. Mom had died a few years before, and I wanted to see my dad on our favorite holiday. I was determined to see him in the morning, but I still needed to prepare my side dish for the dinner I would share with my husband, adult children, brother, sister and their families. Of course I was running late. I'm a "planner" and had meticulously planned every minute of the morning to coordinate all my activities but failed to schedule time for "issues." Suddenly the ultimate planner was having issues!

I was working on the side dish I was slated to bring to dinner along with my fabulous pumpkin pie when disaster struck again. No lemon juice. Crap! We live almost 15 miles from a grocery store, and there was simply no time to make the trek to town, purchase lemon juice, get back to the house, prepare the dish, go see Dad, and get to my brother's in time. Now I know to the untrained eye, this looks far from a disaster, but to a stressed, overwhelmed working woman, this is just the tiny issue that can put us over the edge. To add to my stress, I had chosen a recipe from a friend who had died two years before, as a way of including her in our celebration. So I probably pissed off a dead woman by forgetting the lemon juice. *What was I thinking?*

I took a deep breath and repeated "Life is working for me!" several times until I truly felt a sense of peace and acceptance. I knew whatever came would be perfect for all involved, whether living or dead. Within minutes, my husband, Joe, appeared in the kitchen and asked how I was doing.

I told him my recipe was "ruined" because I had failed to buy lemon juice. He looked puzzled, and then with a gleam in his eye he said, "I'll be right back!"

Within five minutes he was back in the kitchen with *one perfect fresh lemon!*

"It's November in Virginia...where did you get that?" I asked in amazement. He reminded me that my friend had given me a lemon tree the previous April for my birthday. He'd noticed it wasn't doing well in my office and had taken it to his private sanctuary, "Manland," which is a separate building from our house. I never go there - it is Manland after all. The lemon tree had revived, and he'd noticed just the day before that it bore one perfect lemon. I juiced it, and, of course, it yielded *exactly* the amount of juice needed for the recipe. I finished mixing my dish and popped it in the oven while I jumped in the shower to get ready. Another crisis averted! I was really starting to like this "Life is working for me" thing.

But Life was not finished with me just yet.

As I was getting dressed, I noticed my pants were a bit baggy. YAY! I remember thinking that I wished I had a smaller size to try on. Too bad. As I was looking for the perfect Thanksgiving blouse, I noticed a bag on the floor in the back of my closet. What was that? I looked inside and found *three pairs of pants in the next smaller size.* What?! I never bought these and didn't remember where they came from. I quickly found a pair that fit nicely.

Life is working for me, Life is working for me. I repeated it over and over as Joe and I drove to see my dad in his new "home." While the visit was far from the holidays I remembered in the past, I can truly say I enjoyed it. I consciously stayed in the moment with him, where he was mentally and physically at that time, and accepted it for the gift that it was: another Thanksgiving with my dad.

The rest of the afternoon flowed beautifully, and we had a fun day feasting with family, laughing and telling stories that began with, "Back in our day..." to our adult children. As I related my amazing few days to my sister, she reminded me that she'd given me the bag of slacks a year earlier. I'd totally forgotten! The news just added to the magic of the day.

A free pumpkin pie, a lemon, and even smaller pants couldn't beat the miracle of accepting my dad where he was and truly being grateful for the gift of another day with him on the planet.

I get it. I really get it. Life IS working FOR me, and whenever I open my eyes, I see it in action. Life is working for you too. And each of your family members, and your neighbors, your boss and every single person who is currently feeling frustrated by life. They just don't know it yet.

Now will you have pie, lemons and pants magically appear just when you need them? I'm not sure of that, but I am sure you'll handle any situation better when you remember "Life is working for me." And yes, even painful and challenging life events will be easier to weather.

Remember to Remember

So how can you remember that "Life is working for me?" Begin by saying it over and over as a mantra or affirmation. Say it in the morning when you get out of bed. Let it be the last thought you have a night and repeat it as many times in between as you can remember throughout the day.

Keep a note taped on your bathroom mirror. Make "Life is working for me" scroll across your computer screen. Put the phrase in your car where you'll see it often. The key with this concept is to accept that life is working for you and everyone else without trying to figure out the *how.* That's not your job. Yours is *to trust* the Divine Source that creates life itself, makes the sun rise, the tides come in and the flowers bloom is orchestrating all on your behalf whether you understand it or not.

When you trust that all is ultimately working for your benefit, your perspective instantly changes. You relax. You can weather situations more easily and with more clarity. Instead of feeling like a victim, you open up to possibilities. Again, believing life is on your side doesn't exempt you from sadness, grief or tragic events. It does help you see with more loving eyes, hear with more loving ears and feel with a more open loving heart.

Life is working for me. What a concept!

Chapter 5

WHAT DOES LOVE LOOK LIKE HERE? HOW DOES LOVE MOVE ME FORWARD?

W E ALL DEAL with harsh life lessons like feeling alone, nursing a broken heart, dealing with grief, losing a job or facing serious health issues. Life can be frustrating.

I've learned some life lessons the hard way over the years, and remembering to ask myself *"What does love look like here?"* and *"How does love move me forward?"* has been one of my most challenging lessons. It's certainly one of the most rewarding.

I've heard of this concept in many forms, but this simple query has stuck with me as a way to avoid falling deep into anger, frustration and resentment. In challenging situations I ask myself, *"What does love look like here? Love for myself and love for others? How does love move me forward?"* As I ponder this, many answers come to mind, and I can quickly tell which come from my ego and which come from Divine Source. The answers from Divine are simple, clear and direct. They may be firm and persistent, but the energy around them is calm and loving. Answers from ego are different. These can be delivered with anger, panic or self-righteousness. Ego answers often are rooted in fear.

While I've actively used this query for many years, it took being an observer to really understand the meaning of this practice. I got to see firsthand what love looked like when the husband of a couple I knew passed away at home after a long illness. I'll call them Jim and Linda. Let me explain.

When she knew Jim's time was short, Linda asked me to come by the house. It was here I witnessed a pivotal lesson about what love looked like at work in the world. I arrived at their house and was greeted by the family, their faces red from crying. I went into the back room to see Jim lying in a hospital bed, surrounded by equipment. He was weak with labored breathing but a dim light still shone in his eyes.

I can tell you what love looked like that Wednesday afternoon at Linda and Jim's house. I saw love in tear-stained cheeks, in colorful posters made by the grandchildren, in the gentle stroking of Jim's skin and in loving hands administering Reiki. I saw love in the fussing with the bed sheets, in the loving gestures toward Jim and each other, in the position of the bed so he could see the emerald green lawn and softly swaying trees in the backyard. I saw love in the medications and the essential oils, in the whispered "I love yous" and in Jim's determination to hold on a little while longer. I saw love as patient, kind and sad, but resolved.

As the grandchildren arrived from school, I witnessed love move the situation forward.

We all gathered around Jim's bed, gazing at his face, hands on him and each other. I heard his daughter whisper in his ear.

"We're here, Dad. We love you, Dad. We're all one. We'll always be together." Love moved forward with dignity, grace, respect, strength and surrender. And relief for physical suffering that would soon be over. Love moved with deep gratitude and appreciation to our Creator for a shared life and unique journey.

Jim's breathing became faint, and we watched as he peacefully slipped from this world to the next, totally surrounded and supported by love. It was a beautiful experience. What a privilege to have seen love in action by this beautiful family.

This event was profound. It brought home to me the value of recognizing what true, unconditional love for oneself and others looks like in any given situation. Love for yourself is not long-suffering sacrifice, which always breeds resentment; it's not always having to get your way or even putting yourself first. Love asks us to recognize the Divine Spark within and treat it with the same respect that's given to others. You are no more and no less than any other soul that walks the planet. Period. This is what love looks like.

I noticed what love looked like as my friends struggled through five long months of turmoil with Jim's illness, and I watched as love moved them forward. I was grateful for the opportunity to get this experience in preparation for my dad's last health crisis, which began less than a year later.

Asking *"What does love look like in this situation?"* is a great reminder that any circumstance has many moving parts, and all are to be respected with love. You don't have to pretend to agree with a person or position that you don't care for. I can respect another's right to their own spiritual position rather or not I agree with it. Love uses discernment as a tool for evaluation. Fear uses judgment. Can you feel the energetic difference between the two?

For years my issue was always taking care of others before myself. Like a "good woman," I had a job, took care of two kids, a husband and my house, plus two sick parents. Doesn't every woman do this? Many do, which is why women now have a growing number of stress-related illnesses like cancer, heart disease and stroke. While I thought I was being a loving wife and mother, sacrificing my health and mental state just made me morph into a crazy woman. Realizing that true love includes a healthy respect for my own sanity and my body ensured I had the energy and stamina to give *to others as well* as myself in a healthy way. Remembering to ask *"What does love look like in this situation? Love for me and love for others?"* helps keep me grounded in reality and definitely keeps me from wanting to slap somebody. It helps me choose love.

The important question that follows is *"How does love move me forward?"* I'm embarrassed to admit that I know how resentment, anger and jealousy move me forward. I've been shoved, prodded and pushed by those emotions many times and always with disastrous results. Go figure. But how exactly does love move you forward?

How to Recognize and Move Forward from a Loving Perspective

When I find myself in difficult situations, under stress with confused thoughts, my inner wisdom tells me to "ask the questions" we've been discussing here. I promise even if you take only a few minutes, this exercise can help you dissolve anger, move past fear and give you clarity in the situation at hand. Give it a try. Shut your eyes, take a few long deep breaths, imagine your consciousness in your heart space and ask *"What does love look like in this situation? Love for myself and love for others?"*

Then wait.

You might wait a few minutes, sometimes a few seconds but an answer always arrives. When the answer comes in a calm, peaceful, balanced voice, you know it's from love - to me, the same as Divine Source. When the answer comes with panic, wrapped in drama, "You should" or worse yet, "Why didn't you?," you know it comes from ego. An ego response may be fueled with guilt or fear. That's not love. After you ask the question, trust your first response. No need to overthink the answer. Thinking usually opens the door for your ego, and you're asking love, not ego, for a response. Your first loving response in hand, ask the second part of our question.

"How does love move me forward?" Again close your eyes, take a few breaths, go within, ask and receive your response. Here's where it can get tricky. Your goal is to allow love to move *your actions* forward. Love's response will always be instructions for you. It may involve others, but trust you won't get a message from love saying "Joe should take his head out of the clouds and do what you tell him."

Love does not interfere with another's free will. Everyone has the opportunity to learn and grow, and they do so according to their own unique life path. I had a client who was incensed that his office mate refused to read a book he knew would be life changing for his colleague. It was a great book, but the friend obviously wasn't interested or wasn't ready for that information. I advised my client to make the suggestion and then trust an important seed had been planted. It's up to the friend to take action. Act and move forward from love while you allow others to do the same. They may act or they may not. Remember it's their choice.

Acting from a loving space is very freeing. I used to care deeply what my family did, and now I trust they make the best choices for their own lives. I'm there to offer support, guidance and advice when asked, but I'm free of the worry that plagued me in earlier years. I worried my kids would make mistakes, my husband wouldn't work at the "right" place or my parents would suffer ill health. Going forward in love eliminates worry, which emanates from a place of fear. Fear is the opposite of love. I offer support and opinions - lots of opinions - but I now understand worry is wasted energy.

"What does love look like in this situation? Love for myself and love for others?" and *"How does love move me forward?"* can change your life if you let it. Ask the questions, listen for a Divine response and act. Choose love, and your life will be better and so will the lives of everyone around you.

Chapter 6

LIVING IN THE NOW

L IFE IS MESSY. It can be *really messy*. I've found the trick is to *live in the now as much as possible*. Not always easy, but very doable and very rewarding. Why bother? To find the gifts that are presented to you. Gifts of peace, joy, discovery and many others presented by Divine Spirit.

My dad's significant health issues worsened after my mom died, but we were able to keep him at home for nearly seven years until a serious illness landed him in the hospital. That's when the nightmare began. In the 20 months that followed, Dad was in the emergency room eight times, admitted to the hospital four times and three times had lengthy stays in the local physical rehab facility. We had to move him into a memory support unit in the local assisted living home, sell the family home and eventually bring in the hospice team to help us all inch toward his final transition.

There were many sleepless nights, oceans of tears and months of chest pains as I watched my beloved father slip further into an ever-deepening well of illness. My brother and sister, our spouses and our children all watched in horror as prayers didn't seem to work, medicines failed and alternative methods did not result in the outcome we so desperately wanted. It was easy to feel sorry for myself, see the situation as "unfair and unjust," and allow myself to be stuck in the circumstances that continued to reel out of my control. Hours spent pacing hospital hallways, speaking to medical personnel and sorting through mountains of paperwork only added to my duress.

In retrospect, the mounting pressure came from guilt over what I thought I'd neglected to do in the past or worry over what might happen in the future. Had I really helped Dad understand how important it was to eat healthy and take his vitamins? Did I get him out of the house often enough, make sure he had social interaction? Should I have started the acupuncture sessions earlier? Did I question the medical treatment plan when I should have? Was he going to physically suffer because of something I failed to do or say? Even though my family and I worked together on his care, I was the firstborn and his Power of Attorney. I felt responsible. I wondered if I could survive the stress. I decided to look at the situation in a different way.

If Life is working for me, then what was the message in Dad's ongoing health drama? What gifts could I uncover if I looked?

While it's prudent to be mindful of the past and ready to step into the future, the real beauty of life is in the NOW.

I learned to live in the now while spending time with my dad just as he was at any given moment. No, Dad wasn't the brilliant entrepreneur I'd grown up with, but he was now softer, and depending on where he was in his process, utterly charming, funny and quite witty. He was usually the darling of whatever medical team had charge of him at the moment due to his sweet nature and sly smile. This was not the dad I had known. This was a different version of Dad and when I could release my expectation of what he "should be" or worse, what he "was going to be," I allowed myself to thoroughly enjoy him as the beautiful being he was in that moment.

Everyone has their own unique journey. Although I would not have consciously chosen this path for my dad, I came to understand that it's far more loving to respect it rather than fight against it. Yes, I worked with my family to ensure Dad had excellent care and the most optimum healing environment possible. And we worked with his care team to manage his options. But when I consciously allowed Dad to experience his journey without trying to "fix it" or make it the experience I *wanted* it to be, everything changed. Or I should say, *my experience* of Dad's journey changed. For the better. I learned to respect the creative force in my father and trust he was creating the *perfect experience* for him. It was then my job to create my own perfect experience in this situation. I stayed in the "now" of each day and worked to react from that space with love instead of a long laundry list of "what should be" or "what could have been." It was a much more pleasant place to be.

By honoring the present moment, another key truth hit home for me. *Each individual plays a part in the life of everyone they touch.* I've come to understand that throughout his life, Dad has touched many more people than I realized. I always knew how important he was to us growing up. He was everything to my mom and was adored by his friends and extended family. He was a World War II hero, his business fed our family, he was active in local government, served on volunteer boards and supported charities. But that was before. How his Spirit orchestrated things during his last months amazed me.

His critical health situation brought my brother, sister and me closer. My husband and I learned to support and love each other on a level I never knew existed. My adult children grew into even more loving adults before my eyes as they stepped in to help. Dad had enriched the lives of dozens of people who reached out to us to offer assistance or to tell us stories that showed us a side of Dad we never knew. His caregivers, nurses and doctors said seeing Dad was the "highlight of their day" even as his mental and physical state declined. He continued to touch everyone he came in contact with or who knew him through us. It was remarkable.

Even at the visitation before his funeral, my family was inundated with countless stories of what our dad had done for people we'd never heard of. What a gift to choose to be there, in that moment, to receive the gifts we were presented by the visitors that evening. I'm thankful I was aware enough to drink it all in despite my grief. Had my mind been anywhere else but consciously experiencing this gathering, I would have missed the love that was there for Dad and my family. I would have missed the sweet fragrance of the beautiful flowers, the smiles as visitors studied the family photos, the warm hugs, the loving memories of my mom and stories of our childhood. I would have missed it all.

When we dwell anywhere but the present, we miss out on the beauty of everyday life. Don't get me wrong, I'm a huge believer in visualizing what you want and manifesting but not at the expense of the now. I'll grant you it's a bit of a tightrope walk. Just work on getting better at it every day.

Three Ways to Stay in the Present Moment

Here are a few ways that help me stay in the now so I can avoid being haunted by the past or worried about the future.

Connect to Your Breath: Close your eyes, if practical, and take a deep breath through your nose to the count of five. Hold for a count of five and slowly release all the air in your lungs to the same count. Do this three to five times, then silently focus your attention on your normal breathing pattern for a couple minutes. Concentrating on your breathing for even a few minutes will help pull you from distracted thoughts and allow you to focus with clarity on the present. While there are many examples of fantastic breathing exercises, I find this one to be fast, easy to remember and very effective.

Be Mindful of the Present: A great way to be in the "now" is to concentrate on your experience of the present moment. This is similar to the mindfulness meditation technique in that you concentrate on your physical experience in the given moment. Shut your eyes, take a deep breath, relax and silently note what you perceive with each of your senses. With eyes shut, notice what your body is feeling inside and out. Is your stomach rumbling? Any aches in your joints or do you feel wonderfully relaxed? What's the air temperature on your cheeks? Can you feel the weight of your body resting in the chair? Now concentrate on any and all sounds you're aware of. Notice the hum of electrical motors, the hum of distant voices - no need to distinguish words, just the general sound, maybe the roar of a passing truck? What do you smell? Fresh coffee brewing, stale diapers or maybe new snow? Any specific taste you're aware of? Lastly, open your eyes and thoroughly drink in every shape, color and hue of the objects and people around you. Look as if you see everything for the first time.

Do this without judgment. Refrain from thinking "that's beautiful carpet." Rather study the shape, notice the depth of the pile or perhaps how the fibers become a bit matted as people walk across the surface. Look at the richness of the colors and notice the depth of the various hues of green. In this exercise I like to imagine I'm a world class detective examining a scene and digesting every detail for later analysis. This entire process need take only a few minutes, but if done correctly, the effect will be profound.

The Sudden Splash: All of us sometimes get stuck in "patterns" that need to be quickly interrupted to create the energetic space for the desired change to occur. Have you ever seen a neighbor pour cold water on fighting dogs to break them up? That's called a "pattern interrupt" and it's highly effective. I've heard of moms who sent their kids to take a cool bath or shower after a heated argument. I once saw a famous speaker splash water in the face of a participant who was on a 15-minute "whiney road," not allowing anyone else to speak. She was mad, but shut up long enough for the speaker to make his point and help the woman see the situation in a new light. The sudden splash works whether you're splashing cool water on your face or jumping in the shower. Water seems to have a magical power to connect us with our bodies and bring us into the present moment. Cold temperatures can work wonders as well.

If a shower or splash isn't practical, try holding an ice cube or put your hands around a cold beverage for a few seconds. Open your refrigerator freezer and put your face close enough to feel the cold. Step outside on a chilly day and instantly feel refreshed and awake! Whether it's water or temperature, use this method to quickly and easily snap back to the present.

Consistently living in the present moment takes practice but the rewards are great. Understand the past, be prepared for the future, but relish the present and gratefully accept the riches presented in the here and now. It's a great way to choose love.

Chapter 7

RELEASE, RELAX AND ACCEPT

T HESE THREE LITTLE words are powerful: release, relax and accept. Sounds good doesn't it? Like it's easy to release, relax and accept all the crappy things that happen in life and skip down the garden path with a big fat smile on your face. Right. It just seems so much easier to hold on to those resentments, keep bitching and resist letting go of the issues. If you choose to keep complaining, count on staying miserable, and look forward to probably developing serious physical issues. *Or you can choose* to change your attitude and choose love, despite what may appear to be the most unfortunate of circumstances.

Why Release

Learning to release the past as well as judgments about things I couldn't change has been a liberating experience. Let's be clear. If there's a problem or issue you can change for the better, do it. What we're discussing here is the tendency to be haunted by past problems or events that can't be changed or choosing to worry about future events that haven't happened yet - and probably won't. With practice, you can change the way you think about these issues.

I find people often choose to hold on to issues or opinions because they love being "right." They value the feeling of being right above all. Thinking you're right might help you feel superior to everyone else, but you'll find you're all by yourself up on the mountain of "I'mrightdamnit." These "I'm right" folks are some of the loneliest people on earth. Releasing the need for judgment frees you in ways you can't even imagine. Think of the difference between a mountain goat that can enjoy the view from the summit peak and the eagle that can soar high above it all. Releasing the need for judgment helps you soar.

I agree with Vianna Stibal, founder of ThetaHealing® that some of the most destructive energies to the health of the human mind and body are the unholy triad of resentment, regret and rejection. Holding on to these emotions wreaks havoc on your physical body and can create years of emotional pain. Learn to release. These energies spring from some sort of judgment about a past event, person or issue. Let them go.

I had a 45-year-old client once who was still harboring deep resentment toward a long dead relative who had molested her as a child. While years of therapy had definitely helped, she could still be triggered by news stories of abuse. The resentment was a constant torment and led to a deep depression and serious health concerns. She decided to forgive. Once she truly forgave her abuser and released her resentment, her life changed immediately. She felt free. She got a new job. Her health improved. She began dating her "dream man" and enjoyed the loving romantic relationship she never thought possible. Her life improved because she chose to let go of the resentment that had held her prisoner. Forgiving her abuser didn't mean she condoned the behavior, only that she now refused to continue to be a victim. She was finally free.

Releasing judgment about what was happening to my dad at the end of his life changed mine. I finally realized everyone has their own unique journey. I certainly had been teaching this for years, but weary from hours of stress and using these techniques, I finally understood this truth at a soul level. Although I would not have chosen this path for my dad, I came to understand that it's far more loving to respect it rather than to fight it.

In the end, I was able to allow Dad to experience his journey and trust it was the perfect experience for him. And I realized I had to release all expectations of what "perfect" looked like.

Why Relax

I've spent most of my coaching career telling others to relax, urging my family to relax and touting the physical and emotional benefits of relaxation. I know all this stuff. What I never understood was *how to relax*. I read the books, listened to the audios and got body work done, but I know while I was engaged in each of these activities, I was silently figuring out what time it was and what was the next item on my "to do" list. I was anxious to check "relax" off my list and get on with my day! Not the way to relax. I remember thinking for years that I'd relax after the kids left for college, my parents' health improved, when Joe and I retired. You get the idea. It took years of constant stress for me to personally understand the power of relaxation.

I'm not a medical or healthcare professional, but I know the effect relaxation has on my own body. When relaxed, I eat less, enjoy a great night's sleep, am flexible in mind and body and have a playful, fun attitude about most everything. I'm happy. I enjoy everyone and everything. Life is good.

I use this example to help my clients understand what I mean. Put this where you can see it and stretch out both your arms straight in front of you. Now make a fist with both hands and squeeze tight. Squeeze twice as tight. Tighter still. Good! Now feel the energy concentrated in your hands and forearms? Where do you think that energy came from? Not sure? Relax your hands and read on.

I believe there's a specific amount of energy in our bodies at all times to run our physical systems. This energy comes from what we ingest. Brains, cardiovascular and digestive systems need energy to function. Sexual organs, skin and skeletal system all need energy as well. When you consciously directed energy to tighten your fists, you temporarily syphoned off energy from some of those body systems, giving them less energy to use at that time. Holding your fists tight is similar to holding onto the energy of resentment or regret at the cellular level - it makes less energy available to run your normal bodily functions, which may over time lead to serious health issues.

When you hold on to destructive energies like anger, resentment and frustration, there is simply less energy available to be channeled into joy, happiness and health. Make sense? Relaxation on the other hand, allows energy to flow freely and helps distribute energy to the body systems as they need it. In my opinion, that's why you feel so much better, mentally and physically, when you're relaxed. You feel calmer. Usually your thinking is more efficient, helping you make more effective decisions leading to greater satisfaction in all areas your life. Many people think you're even more creative when relaxed. When relaxed, everything is working as it should be.

Why Accept

"Accept" has the following meanings: to take or receive something offered; receive with approval and to agree or consent to something. The energy of "accept" feels gentle and freeing. Some opposites of the word accept include deny, refuse, dispute and reject. Now feel into the energy of those words. They're harsh and combative. The opposite words feel like you're in a fight. That's not the energy you want in your life.

Being able to accept others for whom, what and where they are is truly an act of the heart. Accepting a situation - even one you don't agree with - also comes from the heart. Growing up, I remember so clearly my eighth-grade French teacher, who assigned us the classic *Le Petit Prince* by Antoine de Saint-Exupéry. I have never forgotten one of my all-time favorite quotes from that book:

> *"It is only with the heart that one can see rightly.*
> *What is essential is invisible to the eye."*

An idea or theory can be accepted after careful consideration of facts and various viewpoints, thereby being a brain-centered activity. Depending on the topic, the heart may be involved in the process as well. Acceptance of people, animals, of life itself can come from a heart-centered connection that allows Divine Love to flow between all Divine Beings. This is truly a heart-to-heart connection. It's why "it is only with the heart that one can see rightly." And seeing with the heart helps you choose love.

"Accepting" in a scenario where you may not agree with the issue means you accept that someone has the right to their point of view, not that you agree with the point of view. You can consider facts about a specific political viewpoint, for example, and discern that this is not, in your opinion, the best option. Even so, you can still accept the fact that someone else considers it a viable option.

Think of acceptance as discernment without judgment. That's all. Learn to accept things around you and choose to react from a place of love instead of judgment. That's the key. Since our internal world reflects our external world, when you find yourself judging others less, you will quickly find yourself feeling less judged.

How to Release, Relax and Accept

Using the concepts already mentioned will help you release, relax and accept. Meditation, a gratitude practice and cultivating a belief that Life is working for you all put you in the space of allowing this to happen. Here are a few other ways I found that contribute to your ability to release, relax and accept.

Work with a professional. There are hundreds of books and CDs stacked in my office. I'm all about self-education and I study on a regular basis. That said, I've always believed there are professionals that can help me with my issues. Why not tap into the knowledge and experience of professional therapists, spiritual mentors, pastors, coaches and healers to help me release my demons? Skilled body workers are trained to help release tension and relax the body. Assess where you need help and what type of professional might be best to work with, and *then make your appointment.* Now. You might use a few different types of professionals.

When my dad was in hospice care, I spoke to a clinical therapist for advice on handling family matters during this stressful process. Life coaches helped me deal with my dad's transition, and a business coach helped keep my business on track since I still had to create income. I used massage therapists, healers, yoga instructors, holistic health counselors and hypnotherapists to help me relax and rejuvenate my mind and body. I worked with a great book coach to complete this book! I wasn't using all these professionals at once, but I was visiting at least one or two each month. No, I didn't have unlimited income. I believe every dollar I spent came back to me five-fold if not in actual money, then in piece of mind. Yes, the cost added up, but I thought *the ultimate cost of not utilizing professionals would be significantly greater* than keeping my mind, body and business in good shape. This was undoubtedly the most difficult time in my life, and I knew I could benefit from outside opinions and insight. The most successful people on the planet seek help from others. So can you. Invest in yourself and you'll see it's smart money well spent.

Use release techniques. There are various methods to symbolically and energetically separate you from the loud memories and constant worries that can hold your emotions hostage. Here are a few of my favorites:

"Writing within the Writing" is a technique taught to me by a PhD in psychology and is one my clients love. I've used this with adults as well as children as young as eight with tremendous success. Here's how it works: When you find yourself angry, frustrated or replaying an unpleasant event or issue over and over in your mind, grab a Post-It® Note or 3" x 3" piece of paper and start to write whatever's going through your head. *"What the hell is my boss thinking? I'm the best thing that ever happened to this place! He must be insane to think I'm going to keep up this pace. This is abuse!"* No censorship. Just get out whatever is playing on the loop in your head. Let your emotions pour onto the paper, but here's the trick to this method. *No matter how much you write, you never use more than one 3" x 3" piece of paper.* Start writing and once you get to the lower bottom right-hand corner of the sheet, go back up to the upper left of that same sheet and *continue writing over the words you just wrote.*

You're "writing within the writing" as you continue to let your thoughts spill onto the paper. After a while, you'll begin to see the sheet is almost totally covered in ink. That's fine. Keep writing as long as the train of thought continues. Once the flow of thoughts starts to cease, take the sheet of paper and destroy it. Create a ceremony. I like to tear it up into small pieces, put them in a small bowl and burn it while saying "I release you and the energy that kept you with me. I replace these thoughts with love." After the sheet is burned, I flush it away. I call this the "burn and flush" method. Some clients like to bury the sheet while others like to burn it safely outside and watch the smoke carry the issue to God. Whatever feels right to you will work just fine.

By transferring your thoughts to the paper, you're really helping to transfer the *energy* of the issue to the paper. Since you're writing within the writing, you can't go back and reread your thoughts which keep your energy clean. I've found clients who use journals to write about problems feel good after they've finished writing initially, only to be upset again when they reread the entry. Destroying the paper further tells your unconscious that the energy around the issue is *gone*. You may have to do this a couple times for the same issue. No problem! This is a fast and effective way to feel better and release the issues that haunt you.

"Give it to God" is a phrase I heard in my church growing up. "Give it to the Lord in prayer" was a line in one of our hymns but only as an adult did this become a clear release tool for me. In years past, I would certainly pray to God for resolution in whatever issue was in front of me, but - since He's busy and all - I'd usually add a few suggestions on how that could be accomplished. I was specific. I remembered something about "ask and ye shall receive" and at that time I was into receiving. Aren't we all at the beginning of our spiritual journey? I know now

that lifting your issue to God in prayer and asking "Thy will be done" is all that's necessary. Since God is in all of us and is always working for our highest and best, *His will is always for our ultimate joy.* Give your problem to God and *trust that whatever happens is for the very best of all concerned.* No need to keep praying about it. God does not have a hearing problem. He heard you the first time.

The *"Pink Light"* is another favorite quick technique for adults and children alike. It's simple and effective. You may have heard individual colors are perceived as visible vibrations of reflected light. Color therapy suggests specific colors can be used to create healing environments, evoke strong emotion and promote play. Pink is thought to be the color of unconditional love and nurturing. Its vibration is very calming. Before I tell you the technique, let me explain further.

Humans use the energy we get from food to run our body systems. I believe this energy also creates what is known as our *auric field,* a pocket or envelope of energy that surrounds the exterior of our bodies. This field can hold emotions and even the energy of past events. We unconsciously "read" the energy of people by sensing the energy that's held in their auric field. For example, have you ever stood behind a stranger in line and felt their tension? You didn't have to be told anything, or overhear them speak for you to feel uncomfortable for no apparent reason. You were reading the energy of their aura, perhaps tapping into the fears or hurt they carry in that field. It works the other way as well.

Remember meeting someone you instantly liked for no apparent reason? You were reading the "vibes" in their aura and connected in some way that your mind didn't consciously comprehend. If you're holding on to the energy of resentment and anger, rest assured it's showing up in your auric field, and other people are reacting to what they perceive. So how does the "pink light" work? When you anticipate an unpleasant confrontation or situation, simply imagine the person, issue or situation surrounded in a beautiful pink bubble of light. Imagine yourself surrounded as well, then watch the miracles happen. This works because you are now offering the energy of unconditional love to everyone involved. I know this sounds crazy - even to me- but it works!

One of my clients had recently married a widower with a 13-year-old son. Try as she might, she was constantly battling with her new stepson over minor issues. Although he had been a strong advocate of the marriage, she now believed he was making her life miserable, and she felt her new marriage was in danger. I suggested she try the pink light. She was excited to tell me about her experience at our next session.

"I can't even remember what started the fight, but we were screaming at each other when I remembered the pink light," she told me.

"What happened?" I asked.

"While he was yelling, I looked at him and imagined he was surrounded in a pink bubble, like a bubble gum bubble," she said. "After another 10 minutes, he stormed out and went up to his room, and I continued to think of him in the bubble throughout that evening," she continued. "Guess what happened? The next day he came out of his room and apologized for the way he'd treated me. He said he understood he was mad at his dad over the death of his mother and that he'd been taking it out on me! Can you believe a 13-year-old boy came up with that? I'm going to use the pink bubble on everyone I know!"

Another client was dealing with a difficult divorce. For financial reasons, my client was forced to live in the home he shared with his soon to be ex-wife while they waited for the property to sell.

"During the week it's fine," he explained. "We sleep in separate bedrooms and because of our work schedules, we never see each other. But on the weekends all hell breaks loose!" He continued, "We usually run into each other in the kitchen sometime in the morning and the fighting begins. Even though we try to avoid each other, we're both hurt and the yelling lasts until somebody goes to bed Sunday night." I talked to him about his own actions, explained the pink light technique and looked forward to seeing him again in two weeks.

"You won't believe it!" he said at our next session. "As usual, we got into a screaming match on a Sunday morning when I remembered the pink light. As she talked, I visualized her surrounded in a soft pink cloud and left the house for a drive. Every time I thought of her, I saw her surrounded in pink and imagined love flowing to her. I had a shock when I got back home," he said.

"What happened?" I asked.

"I came in the door and planned to head straight for my room to avoid another confrontation," he explained. "She appeared in the hallway - very calm - and said she wanted to apologize. She said she was sorry for the way she acted and admitted she was sad we had grown apart, but she realized she was angry at the situation and had been taking her anger out on me."

My client was able to peacefully coexist with his future ex for the next few months until he was able to move out. He was shocked at the power of the pink light but thrilled with the results.

My clients have used the pink bubble in contentious work situations, family dramas and even during holiday shopping with great success. The pink bubble doesn't correct troubling situations; it simply *changes the energy* surrounding them, which often aids in peaceful solutions.

Get support from friends and family. I believe we all can benefit from connecting with supportive family and friends when you're trying to release the past, relax and accept what's going on in your life. Be sure to select positive people to share with. This is not the time to spend hours talking to your sibling who screams and wants to make sure you stand your ground "because you're right."

Choose a compassionate friend who usually makes levelheaded decisions and lives a happy balanced life. The special people in my life were invaluable to me during my dad's illness. My friends were loving, compassionate and available, and I am eternally grateful for their support. I'm so proud of how my family dealt with this issue. Of course we were all going through the same stress, so it helped to talk through issues so we were in agreement on how to handle anticipated situations. We did this by consciously thinking of each other's needs as well as our father's. In essence, we chose to love each other through the crisis.

One of my favorite people on Earth is a lovely friend who hosts a potluck dinner for dozens of neighbors and friends twice a month. During these events, people are *packed* in her house. Regardless of the weather or time of year, people show up to eat, talk, hug and catch up on the local news. These informal gatherings are a treasured part of the local neighborhood. Much to my amazement, when her husband died unexpectedly while they were on a trip, she resumed the dinner tradition within a few weeks.

What? I would have crawled into bed and stayed there for at least a couple months, and no one would have blamed her if she did the same. I asked her if she felt up to the responsibility of hosting the frequent events and her reply was eye-opening.

"Well I could stop the dinners and everyone would understand. I thought about it and realized so many people help with the preparations that it's not so hard for me. And I'm surrounded by people who love me and loved my husband. I need that more than ever right now." My friend is always the first to step in to help others, and I think she was a bit overwhelmed at the love that flowed to her and her family during this time. I saw firsthand how powerful this love was and still marvel at this remarkable family.

Be in the moment. Being able to release, relax and accept are just a few more benefits from learning to be in the moment now. Forget judgment, breathe and concentrate on living in the present. There is a freedom to staying focused on the current moment that liberates you from being haunted by the past or worried about the future. When I'm at home, my favorite way to stay in the moment is to cuddle up with my cat, Rory. Pets are very grounding - calm pets at least - and concentrating on Rory's beautiful striped fur pattern, big green eyes and soft purr always brings me to a place of gratitude and peace. Go out in nature, play with a child or sit and revel in the sounds of Mozart. Be in the moment to release the past, relax into the present and accept the beauty of your life.

As you can see, these three little words are powerful: release, relax and accept. Harness their power using the methods discussed here to help you choose love regardless of the circumstance.

Take Thoughtful Action:
Choose to Live Love

So NOW YOU know how to choose love. You've got techniques to help you turn away from sudden emotions like anger and hurt to the more productive energy of love. You also know how to practice these methods to create a life rhythm that is happy, peaceful and fun. Instead of fighting your way through life, you can now use the energy of love to *flow through* one experience to the next. Yes, there will still be bumps in the road of life, but love will allow you to glide past those hurdles instead of staying stuck.

Think of it like this. Imagine a small stream in the winter. As the temperatures drop, chunks of ice can form in the brook and become stuck on rocks in the stream bed while water can still flow around the obstruction. Energies like anger and frustration are the chunks of ice that stay stuck until they can go back to liquid form and again flow. The power of love allows your life to flow. No reason to get stuck in the "mad." Choose to flow through life and enjoy the ride.

By choosing to live love every minute you can, you create a life that is consciously connected to Divine Source, which is pure love. I understand we're all still "human" and as such are here to experience challenges and grow from them. Use the techniques we've discussed here to enhance your life experience and beautifully connect to other people, this amazing planet and to the exact work you're called to do in this life.

You've learned a lot in this book. You now know that a consistent meditation practice can help you become healthier in mind, body and spirit. Cultivating a grateful heart will open you up for even more to be grateful for. You understand your thoughts create your reality and that you are what you think. You've considered the principle that life is working for you, and you've seen how that belief changes your perception of events. You understand the power of queries like "What does love look like here? Love for me and love for others? How does love move me forward?" Living in the now can not only mean gleaning more enjoyment from the present moment, but feeling free of past issues and future concerns. And finally, you see how choosing to practice techniques to release, relax and accept can lead to a happier, less stressed life. You now understand how consciously choosing love allows you to more peacefully flow through the most difficult life experiences. Now it's time to take these techniques and incorporate them into your daily life.

With these tools in place, go forward and take thoughtful action. Look at each day as a new chance to live love. Some days will be better than others. I guarantee you that even the darkest days will be easier when you use love as the energy that fuels you.

We're funny creatures. We can choose to see devils behind every corner, or we can see angels. Choose to see the angels in your life. Look for them. You'll see the devils simply disappear and no longer be part of your experience. Even if they pop up every once in a while, you'll know how to react. With love. Because like attracts like, the more you give love to others, the more love you receive. The more wisdom you share, the more comes your way. The more love you give in the form of a gentle smile, charitable donation or in service to your neighbor...it all comes back to you.

Thoughtful action is love in motion. Choose love and watch the miracles start to flow.

About the Author

D IANE L. HAWORTH is an intuitive coach, teacher and public speaker who believes everyone should "live their joy."

Although her professional life spanned 30+ years in the marketing field, Diane has always been intrigued with holistic healing, including energy work, nutrition and the power of individual beliefs to influence personal health. She studied various spiritual techniques, coaching methods and energy modalities for over 20 years in search of answers to issues in her own life. After freeing herself from illness, excessive weight and an unsupportive relationship, she wanted to help others find the freedom and happiness she now enjoys. As a result, Diane is passionate about helping those who are ready to transform their lives and attract the joy she feels is our birthright.

Diane specializes in blending traditional coaching practices with powerful energy healing methods to help clients release mental, physical and spiritual blocks to success in all areas of their life.

Diane holds a BS in Mass Communications, an MBA, is a Reiki Master/Teacher and a licensed practitioner of neuro-linguistic programming and worked for many years as a certified Theta Healing® Practitioner and Instructor.

She lives with husband Joe and Rory the cat in the beautiful Virginia foothills of the Blue Ridge Mountains and remains close to their four grown children and extended family. To learn more about Diane and her work, visit www.DianeHaworth.com.

5 Ways to Bring More Love
into Your Life Now

Explore five fast and easy ways to enjoy a happier, joyful life by connecting to Spirit and the energy of Divine Love. Release negative attitudes and embrace love:

- Discover how to dream big and shift to a more positive perspective of your world
- Harness the power of the "I Am" to change your reality for the better
- Explore the many faces of love around you and feel more loved and more loving
- Make peace with your past and increase your ability to love yourself and others
- Connect to nature and feel refreshed

Go to www.DianeHaworth.com to download

5 Ways to Bring More Love
into Your Life Now

CPSIA information can be obtained
at www.ICGtesting.com
Printed in the USA
BVOW03s1832290317
479791BV00001B/3/P